GOATS

BARNYARD FRIENDS

Jason Cooper

The Rourke Book Co., Inc.
Vero Beach, Florida 32964

69555595

Edited by Sandra A. Robinson and Pamela J.P. Schroeder

PHOTO CREDITS
All photos © Lynn M. Stone

Library of Congress Cataloging-in-Publication Data

Cooper, Jason, 1942-
   Goats / by Jason Cooper.
   p. cm. — (Barn yard friends)
   Includes index.
   ISBN 1-55916-093-4
   1. Goats—Juvenile literature. [1. Goats. 2. Farm life.]
I. Title. II. Series: Cooper, Jason, 1942- Barn yard friends.
SF383.35.C66   1995
636.3'9—dc20
                           94-39536
                              CIP
                              AC

Printed in the USA

TABLE OF CONTENTS

GOATS

Domestic, or tame, goats are hardy, hoofed animals that are closely related to sheep. Ancient farmers in Asia tamed the first goats 8,000 or 9,000 years ago.

Today, farmers in North America have more than 3 million goats. They raise goats largely for their milk and wool. In other parts of the world, goat meat is an important food.

This goat kid (back) and lamb are cousins as well as pasture pals

HOW GOATS LOOK

Goats are covered by wool. It may be gray, white, black, brown or a mix of colors. The wool of angora goats is very long and shaggy.

Goats have two-toed hooves — like sheep — and long, curving horns. However, many goat farmers **debud** their goats. Debudding keeps horns from growing.

Goats have short, upright tails and wool beards. Different **breeds,** or kinds, of domestic goats weigh between 20 and 150 pounds.

Farmers debud their goats so the animals can't hurt each other, or the farmers

WHERE GOATS LIVE

Domestic goats live on farms all around the world, except in Antarctica. Many goats are raised on little farms in mountains and deserts. Some tribes of people living on deserts and grasslands move their goat herds as the seasons change.

Domestic goats in North America are usually milked and sheltered in barns. Goats exercise and graze in pastures, or open fields.

Goats are comfortable in rocky,
hilly country

BREEDS OF GOATS

All goat breeds probably began when people tamed Cretian wild goats.

In North America, Nubian, Toggenburg, Saanen, angora and Alpine goats are popular breeds.

Worldwide, farmers now raise about 300 different breeds of goats. Each breed has a different size and thickness of wool. Each breed also gives different amounts of milk with different tastes.

Saanen goats produce large amounts of low-fat milk

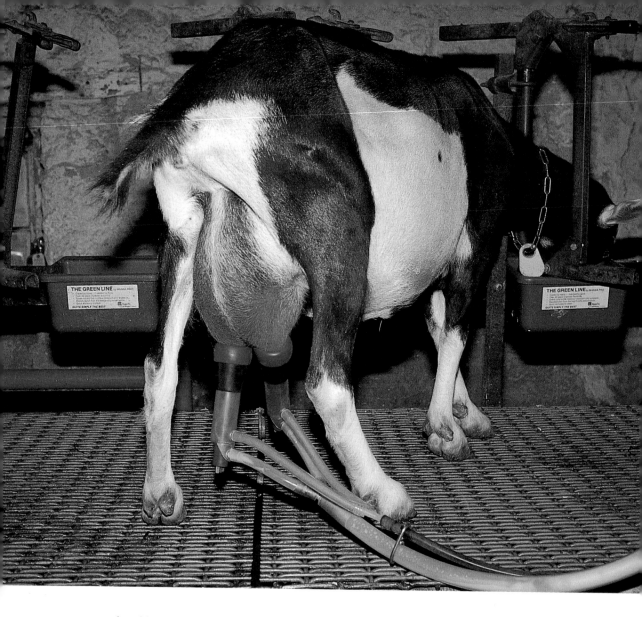

An Alpine goat munches grain while being milked by machine on a milking stand

North America's shaggy, white mountain goats are more like antelopes than "true" goats

WILD GOATS

The Cretian wild goat is one of seven kinds of wild goats. The others include turs, ibexes and the markhor.

Wild goats live mostly in mountain and desert country. They live in parts of Europe, Asia and North Africa. They are very sure-footed as they run and climb among rocks.

The mountain goat of western North America is goatlike, but scientists don't consider it a "true" goat.

This Asian ibex billy's horns dwarf the nanny's

BABY GOATS

Baby goats are "kids." Mother goats, called nannies or **does,** usually have twins. However, a doe may give birth to only one kid — or as many as five.

A goat is nearly full-grown by the time it is seven months old. When a doe is just one year old, she may have her first kids.

Domestic goats can live to be 10 or 11 years old.

A Nubian goat kid's ears flop down, like a lop rabbit's

HOW GOATS ARE RAISED

Most domestic goats in North America spend part of the time in pastures. They munch on grass and other plants. The farmer provides grain and food pellets.

American farmers often raise their goats by hand, feeding them milk from a bottle. This helps make goats very tame and gentle.

Billy, or male, goats are kept separate from nannies and kids. To prevent fighting, farmers keep billies apart from each other, too.

Because her ears are so small, this LaMancha breed nanny looks like she has no ears at all

HOW GOATS ACT

Goats are very **nimble** — they jump and climb easily. Goats climb onto stumps, rocks, and the roofs of their huts.

Like cattle and some other hoofed animals, goats chew a **cud.** The cud is food that the goat has brought back from its stomach into its mouth for more chewing.

A goat farmer visits with her gentle Alpine nanny

HOW GOATS ARE USED

Goats in North America provide farmers with wool and milk. Farmers milk does on platforms called milk stands. A goat gives about 16 pounds of milk each day.

Goat's milk is richer than cow's milk because it has more butterfat. Goat's milk is easier for a person to digest. Many people who cannot drink cow's milk can drink goat's milk.

Some North American goats are used for meat and leather. Goats are also kept as farm pets.

Glossary

breed (BREED) — a special group or type of an animal, such as a *Nubian* goat

cud (KUHD) — food that a hoofed animal brings up from its stomach so it can be chewed for a second time

debud (dee BUD) — the process of stopping horn growth in young animals such as goats

doe (DOE) — the females of some kinds of mammals, such as deer and goats

domestic (dum ES tihk) — referring to any of several kinds of animals tamed and raised by humans

nimble (NIM bull) — able to easily move quickly